BRIAN JOHNSTON

Present Help from Past Writings

Contents

1

Introduction: What Can Go Wrong With Worship?

In the New Testament of our Bibles, the Apostle Paul wrote: *"For whatever was written in earlier times was written for our instruction, so that through perseverance and the encouragement of the Scriptures we might have hope"* (Romans 15:4).

In this series of studies, I'd like us to review some Old Testament narratives for the purpose of obtaining the intended instruction and then to use that for our encouragement in some of the challenges we may be facing today. And some of those challenges will be: 'Should I change church if another seems to be more successful in some sense?' or 'Would my faith survive the defection of a spiritual influencer in my life?'

But first, a word about the Bible. We should read it in one sense just as we read any other book. It's not just another book, of course. Of all the books on our planet the Bible is uniquely a revelation from God. However, the master communicator employed the three universal human writing styles to engage our minds with eternal truths. Someone has assigned each chapter of the Bible to these writing styles and found that the Bible is 44% narrative; 33% poetry; and 23% discourse. It's good to be aware of these different styles within our Bible. As far as reading skills go, it's our awareness of how the Bible is divided into narrative, poetic and discourse writing styles that's likely to help us most in making sense of what we're reading.

First, we need to **see** what's actually there in the text and not what's supplied by our imagination. Second, we need to **understand** what we see as it was understood at the very first time it occurred. Third, we're then faced with identifying the **shared truth** it teaches so that we might **respond** as intended. We want to stress the key point of 'shared truth.'

It's this idea of shared truth that's key to successful Bible study. If we don't pay sufficient attention to this, we'll run the risk of 'proof-texting.' By that we mean lifting and twisting a Bible statement to superficially support our own opinion. Another error we may commit is to 'over-spiritualise' a text. That is, we view the plain text as a type of spiritual code. Now, place names in the Bible do have associations; there's some symbolic force in certain things (such as snake and lion) and some numbers (e.g. 7, 12, 40) appear to serve as imagery. However, with the exception of figures of speech and Bible types (or 'prophetic symbols'), we're not intended to look for hidden meanings by reading between the lines of the text. Nor are we meant to allow our own 'nice thoughts' to control the text. Augustine once famously treated the parable of the Good Samaritan as an allegory, and I've heard the inn spoken of as a church of God! Don't differences between believers often come down to flawed Bible study?

So far, we've identified the three styles of Biblical material: narrative, poetry, and discourse. We've also majored on the chief goal of Bible study and stated that it's to arrive at finding the eternal truth being intentionally shared with us. We now need to put these two things together: for each style there is a specific approach to get at the truths being shared.

Narratives share truth in a particular way. They have distinguishing features: the setting; the characters; and a developing plot. Pay attention to these. A place may have a stigma attached to it. The timing may be in a time of famine. Characters may be painted as foolish, lame etc. Plots often feature conflict and resolution. Narratives don't tell us, they show us. We may ask: 'Does the author interpret what's happening for us or does he pass any form of judgement? Depending on whether traits or actions by the characters are approved or disapproved, we learn to follow or avoid similar examples. Should there be no explicit judgement stated, we can go to clearer texts where the same action is commanded or prohibited elsewhere. And if there's not even guidance anywhere else, then we take it simply as what happened, but not necessarily what should have happened. Let's now put this approach to the test, as we take the example of Israel's first king, king Saul.

"Samuel said, 'Is it not true, though you were insignificant in your own eyes, that you became the head of the tribes of Israel? For the LORD anointed you as king over Israel. And the LORD sent you on a mission, and said, "Go and completely destroy the sinners, the Amalekites, and fight against them until they are eliminated." Why then did you not obey the voice of the LORD? Instead, you loudly rushed upon the spoils and did what was evil in the sight of the LORD!' Then Saul said to Samuel, 'I did obey the voice of the LORD, for I went on the mission on which the LORD sent me;

and I have brought Agag the king of Amalek, and have completely destroyed the Amalekites. But the people took some of the spoils, sheep and oxen, the choicest of the things designated for destruction, to sacrifice to the LORD your God at Gilgal.'

Samuel said, 'Does the LORD have as much delight in burnt offerings and sacrifices as in obeying the voice of the LORD? Behold, to obey is better than a sacrifice, and to pay attention is better than the fat of rams. For rebellion is as reprehensible as the sin of divination, and insubordination is as reprehensible as false religion and idolatry. Since you have rejected the word of the LORD, He has also rejected you from being king" (1 Samuel 15:17-23).

The setting is that Israel's first king, Saul, has been sent on a mission by God. It's a time of war, and God is seeking vengeance on his people's long-standing enemy. The instruction given Saul was quite explicit: he was to completely eliminate the enemy. The developing plot is that Saul has not obeyed that command to the letter. Samuel is the old and faithful prophet of God who holds the king accountable for sparing and bringing back the enemy king and the very best of the enemy's cattle. Samuel demands a reason for this disobedience. Saul has a defence, of sorts. It is that he or the people have had a better idea, meaning a better idea than God's! They would bring back the best animals to sacrifice them to God. I now want to pick up on the prophet's solemn response to this, he said: "to obey is better than a sacrifice."

Animal sacrifices back then were, of course, the appropriate way to worship God. Worship is excellent, but the prophet had to remind the king from God that there was something that was even more important to God than a worshiping people – and that was an obedient people,

people who carried out his simple instructions. A desire to worship is commendable, but not if it involves us playing fast and loose with the instructions and the teaching God has given us.

Today, many Christians would associate Christian worship with what may be called contemporary worship music. In itself, that's not a bad thing, and could even be a good thing. But a philosopher, Andrew Fletcher I think it was, once said: 'Let me write the songs of a nation. I don't care who writes its laws.' Do you see what he was saying? He was implying music is highly effective in promoting ideas. A set of lyrics with a catchy tune that loops around while stuck in people's heads is more influential than a big book of rules stuck on a shelf.

There's a strong following within youth culture of a way of 'doing church' or worshipping that might be described as taking place in a nightclub ambience. More commonly, it may be a worship band on a stage at the front of the congregation. The congregation appreciates the professionalism and the music lifts their mood. For many, if not all, the desire to exalt God is honourable and healthy. Even if the lyrics aren't deep, they pass a doctrinal sniff test. But what background ideas are sometimes being promoted? As Christians, we're intended to exercise discernment. Music, even so-called worship music, can at times become a powerful way to promote and make popular extreme and damaging interpretations of the Bible.

Lively singing is good. It's great to praise God with all our heart and soul, but also with our mind. We should always have our mind engaged. One church leader who's closely connected with the promotion of some very popular contemporary worship music – music that's sung by tens if not hundreds of thousands is on record as saying that Christ 'laid his divinity aside.' I do hope you'll agree with me that this is a totally wrong understanding of Philippians 2:7 where it says that Christ 'emptied himself.' Having reduced Christ in these terms, makes it possible for some to claim that we, too, can live in the same way as Jesus lived – even with God's ability to speak things into existence – to 'name it and claim it.'

In this false way of interpreting the Bible, people come to see themselves as 'little gods.' It's traceable back to the view once promoted that the believer 'is as much the incarnation of God as Jesus Christ was.' To all who love their Bibles and reverence the Lord, this is shocking heresy. A disciple in the Word of Faith Movement that resulted quotes our Lord as saying 'I AM' before he blasphemously adds and '… I am too.' This false teaching says 'Jesus is the first person ever to be born again' out of the pit of hell after Satan had conquered him on the cross. Let me make it clear that this is seriously wrong teaching, even if crowds of people follow its promotional music today – some of them, it must be said, follow it blindly. Saul, too, was misguided or deceived – worshipful sacrifices that involve rejecting the plain teaching of God's Word can never be acceptable to God. Worship is more than the lips, it's about the heart. We're not to let our feeling override our thinking or worse still just think with our feelings. To obey is better than a sacrifice. And pure teaching is better than a catchy tune.

Let us be careful to check out the background biblical thinking behind the messages promoted by some of the 'rock star' pastors who pack vast auditoriums and endorse one another by sharing platforms. Don't forget that our copyright revenue may be going to support seriously false doctrine hidden away in their doctrinal statements, and it could turn out that we're financially supporting an active proselytising cause today, one that at root is rank heresy. There again, there are 'worship songs' so vague that, if taken out of context, it's simply not possible to tell the difference between singing to God or to our significant other: these songs confuse romantic love with Biblical love.

2

Saul: Why Do Some Prayers Seem to Go Unanswered?

The first ever king of God's Old Testament people, Israel, was a man called Saul. Saul began well but became a backslider away from God. He dies tragically as someone out of touch with God. He was so frustrated with the fact that God was no longer answering his prayers that he did something very wrong, something that God forbids in the Bible. What was it? He consulted the spirit world through a medium. You can read about this in the 1 Samuel 28. Saul never did get to the root of his unanswered prayers but we, the readers, can solve his problem. What's more, we can find encouragement to solve our problem with unanswered prayer as we use Saul's poor example as a starting point.

In any time of crisis both Christians and non-Christians turn to prayer. But how do we know that God hears us? How do we handle it when it may seem to us that God has turned a deaf ear to us? As we begin to discuss that, first of all let me ask you to imagine that you're walking down the street one day when a total stranger comes up to you and asks a significant favour from you, maybe asking for a bit of cash. At the very least, there's a sense of social awkwardness, isn't there? Why is that? It comes down to the disconnect between the request and the relationship. It could well be something you'd entertain for a close friend, but for a total stranger? It's awkward and, as we say, jarringly inappropriate. It's that disconnect – the absence of relationship – that makes it like that.

Keep that analogy in mind, but before going further with the issue of prayer, it's surely worth asking ourselves: 'What's the present state of my relationship with God? Are we close?' When Jesus was asked by his disciples in Luke 11:1 about prayer, he taught them a guiding model that began by addressing God as 'Father.' In other words, we're to come to God as his children – which immediately raises the question: How then do we become a child of God? John 1:12 explains how – it's by receiving Christ by believing on his name.

Now as God's child, based on claiming that biblical promise, we'll find we want to read God's Book, the Bible. We'll also find a desire to speak with God in prayer about what we find in his Book – which isn't always easy to understand, definitely not at first. It won't take long before we realize that God answering prayer is not like an indulgent earthly father writing blank cheques! We'll even read in our Bible that there are times when we're not to pray (Jeremiah 14:11). And we'll discover there were great characters in the Bible whose prayers were answered with a "no" (it's still an answer!). These include:

- Abraham regarding Ishmael, (but Isaac was given, see Genesis 17:17,18);
- David regarding the survival of Bathsheba's first child (which died, see 2 Samuel 12:16-18);
- Elijah who asked to die, but never did, (see 1 Kings 19:4); and
- Paul, who 3 times requested the removal of his 'thorn' (seemingly some unspecified chronic complaint – but no improvement was

noted, only an explanation given for its existence, see 2 Corinthians 12:8,9).

In some cases, the answer to prayer was delayed, as if God had said 'not yet.' We've already mentioned Abraham. He's an example of this, having waited 25 years for the birth of his longed-for son. But we'll also find it recorded that there were times when God refused even to hear a person's prayer (e.g. Jeremiah 7:16). At times, the writer of a psalm made the appeal to God: 'Don't go deaf on me!' (Psalm 28:1).

Well, how can we do our best to avoid that unhappy outcome? It would seem that the Bible itemises at least 18 conditions or qualifications that must be met before prayer can be answered:

1. We must ask according to God's will (1 John 5:14; James 5:17).
2. We must ask in faith (Mark 11:22).
3. We must ask after forgiving others (Matthew 6:14).
4. We must not ask for the wrong reasons or with questionable motives (James 4:3).
5. We must ask on the basis of God's mercy and not our own righteousness (Luke 18:9-14).
6. We must ask through Jesus Christ (John 14:6, 13, 15-16; 16:23).
7. We must have right relationships, so that our prayers are not hindered (1 Peter 3:7).
8. We must have no iniquity (sin) in our heart (Psalm 66:18). This, of course, is where king Saul failed if we think back to our opening comments and our brief mention of an Old Testament narrative we're to learn from.
9. We must pray in the Spirit (Ephesians 6:18).
10. We must pray with all perseverance, steadfastly, at all seasons, without ceasing (Ephesians 6:18).

11. We must be 'remaining in Christ' (that is, enjoying communion with the Lord; John 15:7).
12. We must have God's word abiding in us (John 15:7).
13. We will "be heard for our godly fear" (compare Hebrews 5:7).
14. We must have no 'idols' (things in our lives which we put in the place of God; Ezekiel 14:1-6).
15. We must be loving one another (1 John 3:22,23).
16. We must honour God with our possessions and give in order for it to be given (Malachi 3:10; Proverbs 3:9,10).
17. We must ask in secret (Matthew 6:5,6).
18. We must pray for others, unselfishly (Job 42).

Of course, none of us as Christians are perfect – only forgiven. But we must sincerely do our best in regard to the above. These are not listed to intimidate us or discourage us! But if we mean business with God, we'll bear them in mind. As we reflect on them, we can ask the Holy Spirit – who lives within every true believer and is our helper in regard to prayer (see Romans 8:26,27) – to impress on our human spirit any particular matter that requires our attention. Notice also Romans 8:34 – Jesus at God's right hand makes intercession for us also. We have two great divine helpers. That makes sure answered prayer is achievable. The Lord has led us to expect it. Nothing is impossible with his help.

Before we conclude this topic, I do think we need to emphasize regarding prayer that the conversation is more important than any particular expectation we may have. Prayer is a conversation with the Almighty! Time spent talking to God builds that all-important relationship with him.

Jesus said: *"If you remain in Me, and My words remain in you, ask whatever you wish, and it will be done for you"* (John 15:7). While we're stressing the wonder of how we're brought by faith into a relationship with God, this is a key verse, shared by our Lord as he prepared his disciples for his physical departure from this earth. What does it mean to 'remain in Christ' or, as older versions say, 'abide in Christ'? Perhaps, we have the impression it's some kind of mystical experience? Well, this verse links our abiding in Christ to nothing more than simple obedience. For what Christ went on to talk about immediately after commanding us to abide in him, was about being faithful to his Word, and for us now that's the Bible – but also about cultivating the habit of prayer.

And notice, it's answered prayer. It's prayer that's answered because the condition of abiding has been satisfied. We're back to what we spoke about earlier when we shared the illustration of the stranger and the close friend, in turn, approaching us in the street and asking a favour from us. We said we'd more likely give to our friend. We'd find the stranger's request socially awkward. We then challenged ourselves by asking how close are we in our relationship with the Lord. We're thinking of this in relation to our approach to him to ask for things in prayer. When we ask how close are we to the Lord this is really no different from asking are we abiding in Christ? If we are, our prayers will be answered. All the other conditions are met if we're abiding in Christ. For then we'll not be cherishing any known sin, and we'll be asking for things we know to be his will for us.

Talking about God's will, don't be put off by the thought that God already knows what he's going to do. We might know what our spouse or parent is planning to do for us on a daily basis, but it's never wise to take it for granted! It's respectful to discuss things. In all our ways we're to acknowledge God (Proverbs 3:6). It's so rude not to acknowledge someone's presence, isn't it?

3

Jotham: How to Live an Unblemished Life?

The question we'd like to search the Old Testament for help on in this study is: 'how can I be blameless before the Lord at his coming judgement-seat (1 John 2:28)?' By God's grace, we are assured of eternal salvation through faith in Jesus as our personal saviour. But the Apostle John did write about the solemn possibility of our being ashamed before him when we meet him due to not having lived the Christian life well. How may we avoid this?

Well, here's another question, if I may be so bold? It takes us back to the Old Testament and it's purely factual. If I were to ask you which of the kings of Judah (or Israel) has no fault laid to his charge in the Bible, would you immediately respond and say 'Jotham'? If you did, let me confess at once that you're ahead of me there! I read about his life again recently and registered that fact more clearly than I recall doing so before. Yes, the so-called high places weren't removed, and God did bring about enemy invasions, and yet no personal criticism that I could find was levelled at king Jotham. When you think of some of the other more illustrious names, this is quite remarkable. This is of interest to us because we all have an eye on the judgement-seat of Christ, I'm sure, and so would want to learn from Jotham.

One thing it says of him is this – that he ordered his ways before God (2 Chronicles 27:6). I assume that means that he must have lived his life consciously and carefully before God from day to day. Also, immediately before we're told this, and so possibly relevant to it, we're told that he repaired the gate between his house and God's House (check out 2 Chronicles 23:20). Nearness to God, and familiarity with God's House, sounds like a recipe for a life well lived! This was written for our encouragement (Romans 15:4), and after we study the secret of Jotham's life, I'd like us to come back to revisit our original question.

The Bible tells us that king Jotham became mighty. This is clear from the fact that he built towers, and fortified cities, and conquered his enemies –he also embarked on an expansive building program as well as successful military operations. What's really of interest, however, is how he was able to achieve this. The same secret of his success can in principle be applied in our lives too. Jotham's success was because he prepared his ways before the Lord his God; he ordered or directed or guided them according to the Word and will of God. This led him to live his life with the fear of God always before him.

Not much is written about King Jotham in the Second Book of Chronicles, so it's worth reading it all:

> *"Jotham was twenty-five years old when he became king, and he reigned sixteen years in Jerusalem ... He did right in the sight of the LORD ... He built the upper gate of the house of the LORD ... Moreover, he built cities in the hill country of Judah, and he built fortresses and towers on the wooded hills. He fought also with the king of the Ammonites and prevailed over them ... So Jotham*

became mighty because he ordered his ways before the LORD his God" (2 Chronicles 27:1-6).

That last part is the precious gem we've already singled out – he ordered his ways before the Lord. It's a vital lesson we can take away from the life of this man who attained to greater power because – and another way of putting it is this – he made his ways firm before the Lord. It seems the idea is that he prepared his ways in God's presence, so allowing God to direct and establish his path in life. Little wonder then, that unlike kings before him, he didn't become guilty by falling away into idolatry, or by over-stepping the mark like his father Uzziah before him. As far as the Bible's record shows, his personal life was without major fault, except that we might possibly conclude that he wasn't a brilliant leader because we're told that the people continued to act corruptly, for Jotham didn't go so far as to remove the so-called 'high places' where idolatry was practised. But there's no mention of Jotham himself being involved in idolatry. By ordering his steps before the Lord, he made his ways firm, so that his feet didn't slip into wrong ways.

With Jotham's example in mind, we might make our ambition the same as that expressed in the hymn: "May our ordered lives confess the beauty of Thy peace."[1] 'Ordered lives' – just like Jotham: the king who ordered his ways before God. But what does this really mean in practice? The book of Proverbs shares its wisdom with us here. In the early verses of chapter 16, Jotham's word surfaces twice in the sense of 'established' and 'directed': *"Commit your works to the LORD, and your thoughts will be established. A man's heart plans his way, but the LORD directs his steps"* (Proverbs 16:3-9 NKJV).

This seems to expand helpfully on the process for us. Our part – and we assume it was the same in Jotham's experience – our part is to commit our plans prayerfully in advance to the Lord – and allow him to establish proper thinking in us by means of which our steps – our course of action - can be directed in a way that pleases the Lord. It's an ordered life that glorifies God – not a muddle; and not a life ordered to suit ourselves as far as acquiring wealth and prestige or seeking pleasure is concerned; but ordered – before the Lord – by prayer and by the Word of God.

Obviously, reading the Bible and absorbing God's values plays a big part in this. Using again this same word that was the key to Jotham's success, the psalmist prays in Psalm 119, that great psalm which extols God's Word, saying order or *"direct my steps by Your word, and let no iniquity have dominion over me"* (v.133 NKJV).

So we were right to assume that the study of God's Word, the Bible, as applied to our daily lives was at the heart of Jotham's secret. John Bunyan got it right when he said: 'Either this Book (meaning the Bible) will keep you from sin, or sin will keep you from this Book.' The psalmist was determined the Book would keep him from sin, and so he ordered every step of his life according to what he read in God's Word. That's a terrific example. But, let's remember, knowledge of the Bible won't benefit us until we begin to apply it.

The story is told of four men arguing over what was the best translation of the bible. The first man liked the King James Version because of its beautiful, eloquent language. Another insisted that the American Standard Bible was best because of its accuracy to the original text. A third preferred Moffat for its quaint, penetrating words and captivating phrases. After considering the issue, the fourth man said, 'Personally, I have always preferred my mother's translation.' Tolerating the others' chuckles, he continued, 'Yes, she translated it. She translated each page of the Bible into life. It's the most convincing translation I ever saw.'

The outcome of Bible reading that's life-orientated will be lives that are ordered according to God's Word and will – ordered in personal integrity, as well as ordered in family and home life, in church life, in business, and in all our decisions generally. In that sense we can do as the old hymn says and: "Leave to Thy God to order and provide."[2]

It seems so simple, so simple that we may often forget it or lose sight of it. It's simple, but it was the great secret of Jotham's life. It's the one feature of his entire life that stands out as endorsed by God for each of our lives too. Many books have been written about how to be successful in life, how to be a winner – but this one verse, this single idea about ordering our ways before God is all we really need to know. Doing this may not make us a winner in worldly terms, but it's what we are in God's book that counts – and this truly is the secret.

Jotham is the only king, as we said before, against whom no personal criticism is made (other than the high places were not removed)! He ordered his ways before the Lord. He repaired the link between his house and God's house (by repairing the upper gate). There does seem there could be a relationship between these two facts we're given about Jotham. And all this gives us food for thought in terms of how we can be blameless before God at the judgement seat of Christ when the Lord will review and assess our lives of Christian service. 1 John 2:28 says: *"Remain in Him, so that when He appears, we may have confidence and not draw back from Him in shame at His coming."*

To avoid shame, and instead to experience praise, glory and honour before him at his coming, perhaps we could do no better than to put into practice the secret Jotham discovered: ordering our lives day to day by prayer and biblical meditation, while checking out our familiarity with the Bible's teaching about God's House.

4

David: How to Resolve Marital Conflict?

In this series of studies, we're looking for encouraging help from Old Testament narratives that relate to contemporary issues. With that in mind, we read of a time when King David found himself in an unhappy phase of marriage. The wife concerned was Michal, the daughter of Saul. Perhaps we can use this as an example to explore what help we may be able to deduce on the issue of stress within marriage. In the limited space we have, we'll limit ourselves to two of the major dangers. These are typically reckoned to be: failures in communication and inability to resolve conflict.

"But when David returned to bless his own household, Michal the daughter of Saul came out to meet David and said, "How the king of Israel dignified himself today! For he exposed himself today in the sight of his servants' female slaves, as one of the rabble shamelessly exposes himself!" But David said to Michal, "I was before the LORD, who preferred me to your father and to all his house, to appoint me as ruler over the people of the LORD, over Israel. So I will celebrate before the LORD! And I might demean myself even more than this and be lowly in my own sight, but with

18

the female slaves of whom you have spoken, with them I am to be held in honor!" And Michal the daughter of Saul had no child to the day of her death" (2 Samuel 6:20-23).

This exchange of communications between wife and husband can hardly be described as a healthy conversation! How can communication be improved between spouses? Earlier in v.16, we can read: *"Then it happened, as the ark of the LORD was coming into the city of David, that Michal the daughter of Saul looked down through the window and saw King David leaping and dancing before the LORD; and she was contemptuous of him in her heart."*

Does that not pinpoint just where things began to go wrong? David's wife was contemptuous of him. In other words, she disrespected him. The New Testament tells us (in Ephesians 5:33) that just as husbands are to love their wives; so wives are to respect their husbands. This text reveals how we are wired. Wives want and need to be loved (which is why the command is for husbands to love their wives unconditionally). And husbands want and need to be respected (which is why the command is for wives to respect their husbands unconditionally). In any exchange, if the wife doesn't feel loved and that leads her to criticise her husband, and if, because of the criticism, the husband doesn't sense he's being respected, then that couple are on a downward spiral. David found himself in such a spiral here.

One author has helpfully identified what he calls the five love languages.[3] These he defines as words of affirmation, acts of service, spending time together, physical touch such as hugs, and the giving of gifts. In some African churches, when this was applied, it touched some raw nerves. Very often, in a patriarchal culture, the wives were crying out for affirmation or quality time with the husbands or even the gift of sufficient money to adequately support the children of the marriage. It can be a revealing exercise to have couples attempt to identify their spouse's love language. All too often, they get it wrong! The husband expresses his love by the things he sees himself as doing for his wife, but she identifies being loved with whatever time he may spend with her. Mismatched expectations like this can result in poor communication and that in turn can give rise to tensions. So, how well do we deal with the inevitable conflicts? The apostle Paul gives truly practical help in Ephesians 4:22-32:

"... laying aside falsehood, SPEAK TRUTH EACH ONE of you WITH HIS NEIGHBOR, for we are members of one another. BE ANGRY, AND yet DO NOT SIN; do not let the sun go down on your anger, and do not give the devil an opportunity. He who steals must steal no longer; but rather he must labor, performing with his own hands what is good, so that he will have something to share with one who has need. Let no unwholesome word proceed from your mouth, but only such a word as is good for edification according to the need of the moment, so that it will give grace to those who hear. Do not grieve the Holy Spirit of God, by whom you were sealed for the day of redemption. Let all bitterness and wrath and anger and clamor and slander be put away from you, along with all malice. Be kind to one another, tender-hearted, forgiving each other, just as God in Christ also has forgiven you."

We should point out that these form part of general Christian instruction about relationships, but of course the marriage relationship is included. It seems to me that Paul gives us no less than five examples of how to do it – five areas of our lives that must progressively change if we're to either avoid conflicts starting or at least how to resolve them. In each case, Paul first gives a negative command; then a positive command; and finally tells us the reason behind the change. In other words, five times over, he tells us to stop doing something; followed by telling us what we should be doing instead; and then explains the reason for making that change.

Take the first of the five examples. *"Therefore, laying aside falsehood, SPEAK TRUTH EACH ONE of you WITH HIS NEIGHBOR, for we are members of one another."* It's about no longer telling lies. Telling lies, for many, is a way of life. But it shouldn't be for the Christian. So, the negative command which Paul gives first is that we lay aside falsehood. If we allow ourself to become irritated by our spouse's poor time-keeping, we just might catch ourself saying 'You're always late, never on time! We know why we might say something as emphatically as that, but it's almost certainly not true. And so, technically, it's a lie. What's more it's said to provoke a reaction, one that's most likely to give rise to conflict.

Another relevant area is surely the keeping of secrets from each other. Should there not be total transparency within the marriage bond? The positive command is that we speak the truth to each other. And the reason given for this in the context of our relationships with other Christians is that as members of the Church which is Christ's Body, we're members of each other. How much more so, is this within the one flesh of the marriage bond! Even if the members of our own human body don't communicate properly with each other, we know we soon become dysfunctional.

Coming now to the second strategic piece of advice that helps to de-escalate tensions, we may recall how at Lazarus' grave, Jesus showed not just sympathy and deep distress for the mourners (John 11:33-35), but also a sense of angry outrage ('deeply moved') at the monstrosity of death in God's world. But we're often very different when it comes to anger. So Paul now says: *"BE ANGRY, AND yet DO NOT SIN; do not let the sun go down on your anger, and do not give the devil an opportunity."*

We tend to get angry at the wrong things – unlike Jesus, who always got angry at the right things. That's why Paul commands us not to be sinfully angry. Because God is holy and perfect, his anger is never petty, vengeful, haphazard, or cruel – traits which so often characterize our expressions of anger. Jesus displayed the righteous anger of God on several occasions, but not to avenge a personal wrong and never to justify himself. Reacting in hot frustration to someone's aggravating habits is again almost certainly not going to be an example of righteous anger. It's about us.

Now Paul's positive follow-up command. That was where he told us not to let the sun go down on our anger. In other words, sort things out quickly, before they escalate, and certainly before any bitterness sets in. And the reason given by Paul why we should act quickly? It's to prevent the Devil gaining an opportunity. As our accuser, he'd simply be delighted at the opportunity for reproaching us in this. He'd come back later and tell us 'You're no good, God can't use you. You can't control yourself.' Don't give the Devil that kind of opportunity. Settle any dispute quickly.

"He who steals must steal no longer; but rather he must labor, performing with his own hands what is good, so that he will have something to share with one who has need." This is the third lifestyle issue Paul deals with. Of course, we shouldn't cheat on each other in any sense. When Paul switches now to the positive command, and tells us to perform what is good with our hands, it reminds me of the simple statement which summed up the life of our Lord Jesus: *"he went about doing good"* (Acts 10). He continually

dispensed blessing to others by everything he did. If we could be more like that we'd have joy in sharing with others – which, Paul says, is what it's all about.

"Let no unwholesome word proceed from your mouth, but only such a word as is good for edification according to the need of the moment, so that it will give grace to those who hear." On my travels to the Philippines I see painted on schoolyard walls a version of an old proverb: "The words of the tongue should have three gatekeepers: Is it true? Is it necessary? Is it kind?" – ARABIAN PROVERB. These are three tests we'd do well to apply to what we're about to say in an attempt to filter our speech. Words can so easily be weaponised. We deliberately select words that will have maximum impact, words that will hurt.

But now, let's move quickly on with Paul to the positive command – the one about saying instead those things which are good for edification. Words like: "I'm proud of you", "I knew you could do it", "What a good helper", "You're very special to me", "I trust you", "Well done", "That's so creative", "You make my day", "You really tried hard", "I couldn't be prouder of you." And the reason for replacing put-downs with speech which builds the other person up? It's to 'give grace' to the other person – and so be like Christ, who was noted for the gracious words which just poured from his lips (Luke 4:22) and blessed those who heard.

Finally, Paul said: *"Let all bitterness and wrath and anger and clamor and slander be put away from you, along with all malice. Be kind to one another, tender-hearted, forgiving each other, just as God in Christ also has forgiven you."* The mention of bitterness and slander comes immediately after the command not to grieve the Holy Spirit – implying that unwholesome speech and bitterness are things which grieve the Holy Spirit. You can live an outwardly upright and respectable life, but be consumed with bitterness inside, as I suspect David's wife Michal was. Bitterness grieves the Holy Spirit. Paul's positive follow-up command is to replace the vices of bitterness, slander and malice with the virtues of kindness, tenderness and a forgiving attitude. The reason for us being like this is to be like the God who, in Christ, has forgiven us.

5

Asa: How to Pray?

What is prayer and how does it work? That's a modern enough question, but in keeping with our text from Romans 15:4, we can find help and encouragement from an Old Testament king called Asa. The Second book of Chronicles and chapter 14 says:

"Now Zerah the Ethiopian came out against them with an army of a million men and 300 chariots, and he came to Mareshah. So Asa went out to meet him, and they drew up in battle formation in the valley of Zephathah at Mareshah. Then Asa called to the LORD his God and said, 'LORD, there is no one besides You to help in the battle between the powerful and those who have no strength; so help us, O LORD our God, for we trust in You, and in Your name have come against this multitude. O LORD, You are our God; let not man prevail against You.' So the LORD routed the Ethiopians before Asa and before Judah, and the Ethiopians fled. Asa and the people who were with him pursued them as far as Gerar; and so many Ethiopians fell that they could not recover, for they were shattered before the LORD and before His army. And they carried away very much plunder. (vv.9-13).

It used to be the case that the United States, once the world's undisputed super-power, had a total of one million men and women serving in its army, although it has to be said that fewer than 40% were combat soldiers (and fewer than 40% of those were active). The superpower army of the Ethiopians facing Asa, however, had a full one million combat soldiers in its ranks.

There are five great points that Asa's prayer emphasises. First, he says, *"There is no one besides You."* In other words, Asa begins to pray by recognising the greatness of the one he's speaking to. This is adoration of the awesomeness of the God to whom we are praying. Second Corinthians (4:18) encourages us not to look at the things which are seen. The Bible tells us that's how Moses endured – it was by seeing him who is unseen (Hebrews 11:27). We too walk by faith and not by sight. Asa didn't fix his eyes on Zerah or his million fighting men, but he looked to his God in all his uniqueness, really believing that he's almighty, far bigger than the huge problem confronting him.

Then he says, "*[We] have no strength.*" Asa next confesses their own weakness before a mighty enemy and calls on God in the full realization there's no-one else to help. Prayer is an expression of our dependency. Humbled by our weakness, we come before the sovereign Lord. Next he says, "*...we trust in You.*" That was a prayer of no confidence in themselves, but rather full confidence in God. As with all true prayer it was, as we have said, an expression of utter dependence on God – and God gave them a great victory against overwhelming numerical odds.

Then he says, "*in Your name [we] have come against this multitude.*" Like David the Shepherd boy going out against Goliath, Asa didn't cower away backward. He didn't select reverse gear and retreat. It's this that shows the reality of his faith. In weakness, he went on the offensive, trusting only in God. Finally, he says, *"let not man prevail against You."* This is where he's again like Moses. You may remember how Moses prayed that God would continue to help the people he'd brought out of Egypt. They totally didn't deserve it. But Moses is concerned for God's reputation or at least his perceived reputation. He didn't want it to even look as if God could bring his people out from slavery in Egypt and yet fail to bring them into the Promised Land. Surely, we learn from this the kind of prayer that God honours. The psalmist says in Psalm 79:9 – *"Help us, God of our salvation, for the glory of Your name; And save us and forgive our sins for the sake of Your name."* The bottom line of true prayer is God's glory.

Asa routed the overwhelming might of the enemy. Nothing is impossible with God through believing prayer that's made in his will. Another biblical example that really emphasises the vital role of prayer in any undertaking for God is the case of Nehemiah at the time of the return of God's exiled people who'd returned to rebuild the temple, the city and finally the wall surrounding it. Here are:

"The words of Nehemiah the son of Hacaliah. Now it happened in the month Chislev, in the twentieth year, while I was in Susa the capitol, that Hanani, one of my brothers, and some men from Judah came ... And they said to me, '... the wall of Jerusalem is broken down and its gates have been burned with fire.' Now when I heard these words, I sat down and wept and mourned for days; and I was fasting and praying before the God of heaven" (Nehemiah 1:1-4).

"And it came about in the month Nisan, in the twentieth year of King Artaxerxes, that ... the king said to me, 'Why is your face sad, though you are not ill? This is nothing but sadness of heart.' Then

I was very much afraid. And I said to the king, 'May the king live forever. Why should my face not be sad when the city, the site of my fathers' tombs, is desolate and its gates have been consumed by fire?' Then the king said to me, 'What would you request?' So I prayed to the God of heaven. ⁵ Then I said to the king, 'If it pleases the king, and if your servant has found favor before you, I request that you send me to Judah, to the city of my fathers' tombs, that I may rebuild it'" (Nehemiah 2:1-5).

Nehemiah was indeed commissioned for this task, and once there, he mobilized a workforce: *"So the wall was completed on the twenty-fifth of the month Elul, in fifty-two days"* (Nehemiah 6:15-16). If we were to check out the Hebrew calendar, we would see that the time during which Nehemiah was before God in prayer for the anticipated work was 3 to 4 months; whereas the work itself, once begun, was completed in 52 days. In other words, Nehemiah spent almost 4 months in prayer for the work of rebuilding the wall around Jerusalem, a work that itself took less than 2 months. Doesn't that show us that the most important thing in any work for God is prayer? More prayer, less activity should perhaps be our motto.

We've majored on the battle scene with Asa against the Ethiopians and how by prayer he prevailed. It was the very same in Joshua's day:

"Then Amalek came and fought against Israel at Rephidim. So Moses said to Joshua, 'Choose men for us and go out, fight against Amalek. Tomorrow I will station myself on the top of the hill with the staff of God in my hand.' Joshua did just as Moses told him, and fought against Amalek; and Moses, Aaron, and Hur went up to the top of the hill. So it came about, when Moses held his hand up, that Israel prevailed; but when he let his hand down, Amalek

prevailed.

And Moses' hands were heavy. So they took a stone and put it under him, and he sat on it; and Aaron and Hur supported his hands, one on one side and one on the other. So his hands were steady until the sun set. And Joshua defeated Amalek and his people with the edge of the sword. Then the LORD said to Moses, 'Write this in a book as a memorial and recite it to Joshua, that I will utterly wipe out the memory of Amalek from under heaven.' And Moses built an altar and named it The LORD is My Banner; and he said, 'Because the LORD has sworn, the LORD will have war against Amalek from generation to generation'" (Exodus 17:8-16).

These examples are given to us in the Bible as teaching examples. While Joshua led the army against the Amalekites in the valley, Moses was up on the overlooking hilltop lifting up the staff that was the sign of God's power in working for his people. But lifting up that reminder of their dependence on God's powerful help was, in effect, prayer, as the posture also suggests. It was the activity on the hill that determined the outcome in the valley below. While Aaron and Hur steadied Moses' hands, the Israelite army had the upper hand. But when Moses' hands got tired and came down, the tide in the valley turned in favour of the enemy. With the assistance of Aaron and Hur, Moses' hands remained upheld and so victory was gained.

We might think Joshua did the hard work, but Moses was wearied in prayer. Prayer is hard work. Too often, perhaps, we give up. Our hands are not steady until the setting of the sun. It's certainly good when we have praying partners. And who might we be able to support in prayer today? Every battle we fight, while fighting the good fight of the faith, is the Lord's. Praying didn't eliminate the need for fighting, but for sure the fighting depended on the praying. Moses recognised the source of their victory that day when he build an altar and named it 'The LORD is my Banner.' The word 'banner' means something raised or lifted up, as the staff of God had earlier been. Now the name of God was exalted in victory salute. As an army identifies with its flag, and here it's a flag of victory, so we through prayer identify any victory achieved as rightfully belonging to God.

6

Ahaz: What if Things Look Better Elsewhere?

King Ahaz was one of the worst desecrators among all the southern kings who ever ruled in Israel. What makes him that is the fact that he sacrificed God's truth on the altar in ways we'll explain in a moment. But let's first ask a contemporary question: how do we feel if other types of church are seemingly being more successful than our own? This can be confusing and so it's a question we hope to get help on by referring back to the Bible record of this king.

It certainly was the case back in his day that he felt things weren't working despite the Temple of God that Solomon built still standing in Jerusalem. When the army of God's people was being defeated on the battlefield, Ahaz took a pragmatic view. Sometimes we're all too easily impressed by superficial appearances. Ahaz displays this same tendency – for to him things looked better elsewhere. His neighbours had an altar that Ahaz felt looked better than the one standing in front of Solomon's temple. To that extent, Ahaz was influenced by aesthetics.

There's a widespread view today that we should be free to modernize our ways of serving God and move with the times, or to use an unfortunate phrase that gets heard quite a lot: 'it's time for the church to catch up with the modern world.' Sure enough, Ahaz felt like that too; he felt he should be able to have a say. He ended up making radical changes to the order that God had prescribed at the heart of the temple itself. As we follow the historical case of Ahaz, we'll have the opportunity to watch a worked example unfolding before our eyes, one that lets us track the consequences of pursuing what looks to be more successful or what appears more attractive to our taste or otherwise making adjustments as seems best to ourselves. We can learn from his mistakes.

So, what did this man do? In the poetic language of the Bible prophet, Jeremiah, he abandoned the fountain of living waters and replaced it with a broken cistern. In other words, he ceased to acknowledge and honour the true and living God and adopted for himself the pagan god of a neighbouring country. This is what the biblical chronicler said:

> *"Now during the time of his distress, this same King Ahaz became even more unfaithful to the LORD. For he sacrificed to the gods of Damascus who had defeated him, and said, 'Because the gods of the kings of Aram helped them, I will sacrifice to them so that they may help me.' But they became the downfall of him and all Israel"*
> (2 Chronicles 28:16-23).

The setback he'd suffered in battling Israel's neighbouring states should have made him realize that things were not what they should have been between himself and God, the true and living God. But he did what people often do. He overlooked the possibility that he might be at fault and blamed God for the failure of his people in battle. Things weren't working for him, and obviously things were working for the victorious pagan enemy. Ahaz decided this could only mean that their pagan god was more powerful than Israel's God, the God of their forefather, Abraham.

Before we rush to condemn this man, perhaps we should take a look at ourselves. If the local church that we're part of is decreasing in numbers, and we notice other churches are seemingly prospering, for example in the number of their members, are we guilty of sometimes wishing we could copy their practices and even adopt their teachings which previously we might have felt were questionable from a biblical perspective? When things don't seem to be working, and aren't producing the kind of results we're looking for, do we sometimes feel like trading in our long-held convictions for the latest new spiritual trend or fashion?

Is that important, you ask? Okay, let's put it this way. Imagine you go to a restaurant and order a fillet steak. Thirty minutes later, the waiter returns and puts a pizza in front of you, claiming it's the best pizza you'll ever try. What would you do? I'm pretty sure you'd send it back … because it wasn't what you ordered – not even close. Well, God gave us his 'order' – I mean, he told us exactly how he wanted to be served through his commandments in the New Testament known as 'the Apostles' teaching', but instead of us delivering exactly what he asked for, we all too easily get distracted by thinking about what we want and what others seem to want, and by what's been done traditionally by the generations before us.

The summary of New Testament local church life we find in the seven points listed in Acts 2:41,42 is in agreement with what we find throughout the church history Book of Acts. What's more, these steps were anticipated in principle in the Old Testament (in terms of redemption, baptism and serving according to a pattern of obedience). We also find them performed across the whole breadth of New Testament Christian experience without contradiction. Then this uniform practice gets explained in more detail in the Bible letters that follow. Did you know, there are actually 5,040 different ways in which you can arrange any seven objects in order? But these ordered seven steps taken by the first Christians must be in just the one arrangement that God endorses in the Bible.

We say 'must be in the one arrangement' but among denominations of Christianity we observe a great variety of different permutations, for example some would put participation in so called 'holy communion' ahead of biblical conversion and baptism. In effect, that puts step 6 before steps 1 and 2 if we refer back to Acts 2:41,42. How do we feel about redesigning the pattern of Christian service that God has set in his word? Much more important, how does God feel about it? Reading the history of King Ahaz can help us answer that question.

> *"Now King Ahaz went to Damascus to meet Tiglath-pileser king of Assyria, and he saw the altar which was at Damascus; and King Ahaz sent to Urijah the priest the pattern of the altar and its model, according to all its workmanship. So Urijah the priest built an altar; according to everything that King Ahaz had sent from Damascus, in that way Urijah the priest made It, before the coming of King Ahaz from Damascus. And when the king came from Damascus, the king saw the altar; then the king approached the altar and went up to it, and burned his burnt offering and his meal offering, and poured out his drink offering and sprinkled the blood of his peace offerings on the altar. And the bronze altar, which was before the LORD, he brought from the front of the house, from between his altar and the house of the LORD, and he put it on the north side of his altar.*

Then King Ahaz commanded Urijah the priest, saying, 'Upon the great altar burn the morning burnt offering, the evening meal offering, the king's burnt offering and his meal offering, with the burnt offering of all the people of the land, their meal offering, and their drink offerings; and sprinkle on it all the blood of the burnt offering and all the blood of the sacrifice. But the bronze altar shall be for me, for making inquiries.' So Urijah the priest acted in accordance with everything that King Ahaz commanded" (2 Kings 16:10-16).

If earlier we were in effect asking the question: Should we sacrifice scripture on the altar of pragmatic success? Now, again based on Ahaz' disastrous example, we can also ask: Should we sacrifice scripture on the altar of aesthetics?

One writer (Francis Chan) tells a modern parable when he says: "suppose I was concerned about people's health so I ... rented a building and painted a cool sign with a bunch of happy vegetables on it. I began making drinks by blending kale, carrots, beets, and spinach. My customers loved my drinks and came daily. There was just one problem: there aren't enough health fanatics to keep my business afloat. My solution: whipped cream. Once I topped my drinks with it, more people started coming around. Soon after, I added chocolate syrup and sales grew even more. Once gummy bears and M&M's were introduced, I started making a fortune. I would still boast that my drinks contained some healthy ingredients, even though I knew my clients were getting fatter and more lethargic. My desire to run a lucrative business at some point overpowered my original goal of health. At some point in the process, I should have taken down the sign."[4]

Like Ahaz, we have to define what success is. Prayer, communion, fellowship, and Bible reading don't attract large crowds in typical Western societies. So we start adding elements that do attract people. We accomplish a goal, but it's the wrong goal. Let me remind you: we've been reviewing the career of an apostate King of southern Israel who changed his God, changed his altar and changed the use of the original altar. In surrounding Western secular society, the parallels with Ahaz are even more marked. What we see today, echoes what we read in Romans 1:18-32. Although people know God (with evidence), they haven't seen fit to acknowledge him any longer, but have exchanged the truth for a lie, honouring the creation not the creator, and abandoned the natural use of male and female, in degrading passions and indecent acts, while reaping the due penalty of their error.

Can we not detect the same three stages of downward spiral as with king Ahaz? One, suppress and exchange the truth of God. Two, repeal and redesign his instructions. Three, change the way we use our bodies and suffer the results of unnatural behaviours. In other words, we're told now that the universe created itself, so replacing belief in any supernatural intelligence. Second, we now make our own definitions and rules in such areas as marriage and gender. And thirdly, we now insist there's virtue in living by our own social codes of behaviour, regardless of what God has to say about them in the Bible.

As God's people living in such a hostile environment, are we ready to give up on prayer if it doesn't seem to be working? Ready to reconstruct the local church so as to make it more appealing to those who may start to attend services? Ready to adopt worldly thinking, and the behaviours that invariably follow? Let's instead be sure we learn from Ahaz' disastrous decisions.

7

Joash: What if My Mentor Leaves?

How would we cope if our best friend and a significant influencer in our lives were to suddenly leave our church? Obviously, we'd be concerned for them and try to be understanding about whatever had gone wrong. But would our own personal convictions about the place in which we were serving God be strong enough to survive the shock? This is, sadly, not an uncommon experience – and may in fact be one that you're facing up to right now.

I trust it helps to know that there's nothing new under the sun. It seems that those words from the Bible can find an application here. For among the kings who reigned in Southern Israel was one who arrived on the throne as a mere boy, scarcely more than an infant, really. His arrival unfolded in the most unusual of circumstances. We should revisit these circumstances in order to set the scene for something we can learn from as we grapple with the sort of situation we mentioned a moment ago.

Let me transport you back in time to the days of a king by the name of Ahaziah who once ruled in Jerusalem. In some ways these times were no different from the lawlessness of our own time. These were turbulent days, and when King Ahaziah was killed, his mother did a very wicked thing. She seized the reins of power and set about destroying everyone who had a rightful claim to the throne.

Her fiendish plan was always destined to fail, however, because it was inconsistent with God's supreme plan to bring salvation through a Messiah who would descend from king David's royal line. Despite wicked queen Athaliah's best (or worst!) efforts, namely her attempt to kill all of the previous king's successor sons, one tiny baby son was secretly hidden by means of help from a worthy couple who were the baby's aunt and uncle.

And so baby Joash – a baby son of the king who'd been killed – was hidden away in a bedroom while the slaughter of all the king's other descendants was taking place. And for the next six years he was kept tucked away from view, hidden in God's house, the temple at Jerusalem. This is how the Bible sums it up:

"So he was hidden ... in the house of the LORD for six years, while Athaliah reigned over the land" (2 Kings 11:3 NKJV).

"In the seventh year Jehoiada sent and brought the captains of hundreds— of the bodyguards and the escorts— and brought them into the house of the LORD to him. And he made a covenant with them and took an oath from them in the house of the LORD, and showed them the king's son" (2 Kings 11:4 NKJV).

I find that inspiring reading – the man Jehoida, who was a priest, bringing in the military leaders into the temple and letting them into the secret that for all of those six terrible, dark years of oppression there had been a secret survivor – and that he was the rightful king! How those soldiers must have gasped with amazement, and with relief too, at the sight of the young boy who was born to be king – someone whose existence had been a closely guarded secret up till that moment! And from that moment something like a military-style coup was launched to bring this young boy to the throne.

But let's stay a little longer with that moment of revelation in the temple. It certainly had come as a wonderful revelation to those soldiers: to get a glimpse of the king's son in God's house. I'm pausing with you at this point, because I can't help but see an illustration there of something that's right up to date. Do we not live in a time when Satan has usurped God's rightful place in the thoughts and lives of men and women? Late on in the Bible, the apostle John says: *"... the whole world lies under the sway of the evil one"* (1 John 5:19). They're dark days that we live in, for this controlling influence is nothing but only *"the power of darkness"* (Colossians 1:13). It's tyranny and oppression of a spiritual nature and it's throughout the world system today.

But what a revelation is to be found in our Bibles! There's salvation found in a child born and raised in this world, born outside of the royal palaces of his day and someone whose identity was hidden from all but a few. I'm talking, of course, about Jesus Christ, God's Son and the Saviour God has provided. He's the Son of the King eternal, God (1 Timothy 1:17). And something I've come to understand from God's Word, the Bible, is this – that when we come to appreciate the revelation of Jesus as he stands related to God's house today, then we've come to appreciate the full extent of God's good news for the people of this world. It's something I rejoice in as I share it with you – this vision of the King's Son in God's house.

Jehoida the priest would go on to remain a spiritual adviser to the young king. But Jehoiada, the kingmaker, was of course a much older man, and when he died, Joash seemed to become a different person. The Bible tells us he "did that which was right in the sight of the Lord all the days of Jehoiada the priest." Without the old priest's influence and guidance, Joash, now in his thirties at least (see 2 Kings 12:6,7), began to reverse his earlier reforms. He undid the good he'd done earlier in life. Almost unbelievably, he forgot the kindness Jehoiada had shown him and even had his son, Zechariah, murdered (2 Chronicles 24:22).

So the life of Joash gives us a lot to think about, and leaves us with some personal challenges. Do we attend church services or youth camps only to please our parents? Or have we become less effective in our spiritual service after some influential figure has moved away? By God's help, let's guard against that happening.

The story is told of some young trouble-makers who got off a bus. The driver called out as they were leaving. "Excuse me, but you've left something behind … it's a bad impression!" I mention that because the only possible New Testament reference back to the life of Joash – and it's an indirect one – may be to the messenger he killed (Matthew 23:35; 2 Chronicles 24:20-22). What will we be remembered for? Our works whether good or bad will meet us again one day (2 Corinthians 5:10) when the Lord Jesus Christ will assess the life and service of every born-again believer. Decisions we make now will matter then – and forever.

We've been reading the story of a dependent king, a man who was weak and easily influenced. His stability depended on the influence of one man over his life. And when that man died, Joash fell apart. The Apostle Paul was an altogether different character. He could say in his last biblical letter to Timothy: *You are aware of the fact that all who are in*

Asia turned away from me, among whom are Phygelus and Hermogenes" (2 Timothy 1:15).

In recent history, a female British Prime Minister made famous the expression: "the lady is not for turning!" Well, we could also say: the Apostle was not for turning! Even a mass defection from the Christian faith did not in any way cause him to question his own convictions, as far as we can tell. His tone would appear resolute, as he says to Timothy: *"Hold on to the example of sound words which you have heard from me, in the faith and love which are in Christ Jesus. Protect, through the Holy Spirit who dwells in us, the treasure which has been entrusted to you"* (2 Timothy 1:13-14). The poet, Rudyard Kipling, has famously said "If you can keep your head when all about you are losing theirs … you'll be a man, my son."

So, we return to our opening question – how would we cope if our best friend and significant influencer left our church? Would you be a Joash or a Paul? Whom are you trying to please – other people or God? Do you belong where you worship for social or spiritual reasons? Is your service for God rooted in convenience, companionship or conviction? The Apostle Peter (in 1 Peter 3:15) tells us we ought to be able to personally defend our beliefs. Can we? Or do we just follow the crowd or even one influential person?

8

Josiah: What Is True Revival?

University leaders in the U.S. recently described a phenomenon that started when some students stayed late after a chapel service on Feb. 8, 2023, to continue singing and praying—and didn't leave. Other students joined them over several days that stretched into a week, and then another week. Then the nonstop, two-week prayer session at Asbury University that brought tens of thousands of people from across the country to the Christian campus in Kentucky finally ended. It again raised the question: 'What does a revival look like?' I personally remember being asked this, or a very similar question, at a time when there was a significant response to the message preached in the country I was visiting. I believe we can get insight from the time Josiah was king in Jerusalem.

Judah was a land of images and idols when Josiah began to reign. But he would become a teenage reformer with a zeal to repair the LORD's temple at Jerusalem. The Bible makes special mention of his zeal when it says: *"The king commanded Hilkiah the high priest ... to bring out of the temple of the LORD all the vessels that were made for Baal, for Asherah, and for all the host of heaven; and he burned them outside Jerusalem in the fields of the Kidron ... He did away with the idolatrous priests whom the kings of Judah had appointed to burn incense in the high places in the cities of Judah and in the surrounding area of Jerusalem, also those who burned incense to Baal, to the sun and to the moon and to the constellations and to all the host of heaven* (2 Kings 23:4,5).

That's a horrific catalogue of the extent of the idolatry that was then being practised in and around Jerusalem – the very centre for the worship of the true and living God. The purging begun by Josiah seems to have been the most far-reaching so far, leading us to ask: 'What had produced such a revivalist spirit in the young king?' In young Josiah, there was a heart that trembled at God's Word (Isaiah 66:2). That becomes clear when during Josiah's reforms, the high priest made an astounding discovery. His words are recorded in the Bible in 2 Kings 22:8, *"I have found the book of the Law in the house of the LORD."* Imagine the Word of God having been lost! What would be the king's reaction to this news? Other kings had been indifferent to it – or worse than indifferent. But Josiah:

> *"... gathered to him all the elders of Judah and of Jerusalem. The king went up to the house of the LORD and all the men of Judah ... with him ... and he read in their hearing all the words of the book of the covenant which was found in the house of the LORD. The king stood by the pillar and made a covenant before the LORD, to walk after the LORD, and to keep His commandments and His testimonies and His statutes with all his heart and all his soul, to carry out the words of this covenant that were written in this book. And all the people entered into the covenant"* (2 Kings 23:1-3).

Josiah was absolutely thrilled by this discovery. The Word of God had been found! This was a momentous event. As I read about it again, it makes me think about the Great Awakening we find recorded in Nehemiah chapter 8. That was at a later time in history, after God had swept his idolatrous people into a period of captivity in order to discipline and reform them. By Nehemiah chapter 8, God's people had recovered their land and rebuilt their temple, but their heart wasn't altogether in it. First, God stirred up their enthusiasm by sending the prophets Haggai and Zechariah. Then he sent them Ezra who was a scholarly priest. He was a man of the Book. Nehemiah who came to Jerusalem later, supported Ezra in bringing God's Word before the people. Nehemiah chapter 8 begins:

"And all the people gathered as one person at the public square which was in front of the Water Gate, and they asked Ezra the scribe to bring the Book of the Law of Moses which the LORD had given to Israel. Then Ezra the priest brought the Law before the assembly of men, women, and all who could listen with understanding, on the first day of the seventh month. And he read from it before the public square which was in front of the Water Gate, from early morning until midday, in the presence of men and women, those who could understand; and all the people were attentive to the Book of the Law."

As we think about what revival is, let's observe how this incident started with the invitation given to Ezra to 'bring the Book.' Revival today, as then, will only begin when we're ready to pay attention to God's Word. There's no alternative, and no short-cut or quick fix. Ezra had already been among them for 14 years, during which time he'd set his heart upon studying God's Word, both putting it into practice personally and teaching it publicly (Ezra 7:10). There's a sense of something really solid here. The preacher was a man who'd got to grips with his message from God. These days, aspiring young preachers are counselled not to overdo their opening illustration at the expense of minimising their later treatment of the biblical text. The form that advice may take is: 'Don't build the front porch bigger than the house!' Ezra concentrated on giving the plain sense of God's Word as he preached it – without trying to embellish it in any way.

A moment ago, we saw the text tell us that Ezra 'read' from the Book of the Law (v.3). Don't think for a moment about this as boring, monotonous reading. The word used here to convey the reading of Ezra was the same as the word to describe the proclamation of Jonah in the streets of Nineveh ('cried out' – Jonah 3:2). And that was surely animated! Another piece of modern coaching for wannabe preachers is: "the bland should not lead the bland." Ezra's style of delivery, it seems, was far from bland. It definitely held his audience – for hours! That leads us next to think about the appetite of the audience. In some parts of the world today I'm aware of the audience arriving at 7 a.m. simply so as to be sure of not missing the start of the Bible sharing that was scheduled for 3 p.m.

But it seems that in different parts of the world, elements of some audiences are getting restless after ten minutes. However, one suspects those same people who can't endure more than 10 minutes of preaching may well sit all through a two-hour movie. And that just shows that the problem is not one of concentration but of inclination. We concentrate on what we want to concentrate on.

Although the following information may be biased towards the western world, I was reading recently that in 2020, 300 billion emails were sent and received per day.[5] People also send over 100 billion messages through Facebook Messenger every day. That includes messages sent across Facebook's family of apps (including Instagram, WhatsApp, etc.)

and was dated 26 October 2022. And that's a big part of the problem – we're losing the ability to read studiously at length. We're distracted by soundbites and captions. But meditating on God's Word is the foundational secret for life, and without it there can be no genuine revival. But now, let's read a bit further in Nehemiah chapter 8:

> *"Ezra the scribe stood at a wooden podium which they had made for the purpose ... Then Ezra opened the book in the sight of all the people, for he was standing above all the people; and when he opened it, all the people stood up. Then Ezra blessed the LORD, the great God. And all the people answered, "Amen, Amen!" ... and the Levites explained the Law to the people while the people remained in their place. They read from the book, from the Law of God, translating to give the sense so that they understood the reading"* (Nehemiah 8:1-8).

It makes no difference how long we speak for – or how respectful the audience are – if they have no clue as to what's being said. That's not all down to the preacher – those listening to him have to be 'switched on' and interested in what he's communicating. And that's what was happening here, for we read that the people stood up in recognition of the fact that when the Book is opened, God speaks through his Word. The plain meaning of the text itself is the message. It shouldn't be about our nice thoughts nor speculative spiritualizations in decoding words or reading between the lines and the making of random word associations. True Bible preaching, modelled on what we find here, is Bible teaching that gives the clear sense of the passage itself, the one that's been publicly read. One last part of reading from Nehemiah chapter 8 (9-12):

> *"Nehemiah, who was the governor, and Ezra the priest and scribe, and the Levites who taught the people said to all the people, 'This*

day is holy to the LORD your God; do not mourn or weep.' For all the people were weeping when they heard the words of the Law. ... Then all the people went away to eat, drink, to send portions, and to celebrate a great feast, because they understood the words which had been made known to them."

It's through God's Law or the Bible that the knowledge of sin comes. Awakening is a heightened sense of sin. I can vividly recall a woman in a Far Eastern audience being in tears at the close of the message. She said she'd felt "overwhelmed by a sense of sin." That's also what happened here. They were cut to the core of their beings by the sharpness of God's Word that Hebrews 4:12 describes as being *"sharper than a two-edged sword."* That text also describes the Bible as being *"living and active."* So, it's wrong to say a preacher brings the text to life. The Bible doesn't need to be brought to life – it's already living. Ideally, it energizes his sermon. Of all things, the Bible is the thing that's truly 'cutting edge.' It strips away every fig leaf of our attempted cover-up. Our lives at their most vulnerable are exposed to its sharpness. So, in answer to our question of 'What does revival look like?' we've seen it begins and ends with the impact of God's Word on our lives.

9

Amaziah: 'Is It Worth It?'

Have you ever wondered: 'Is serving the Lord really worth it?' Or 'Do I really need to surrender everything that others seem to enjoy and get away with?' We'll turn to another Old Testament king to be guided by the example of his life. King Amaziah was someone who for a while at least did the right things, but he didn't love God with all his heart. While Amaziah is commended for doing what's right, he's not compared with king David, but is instead contrasted with him. David is always mentioned as the gold standard by which all others after him were later judged. The Bible tells us:

"Amaziah was twenty-five years old when he became king, and he reigned twenty-nine years in Jerusalem ... He did right in the sight of the LORD, yet not with a whole heart ... Moreover, Amaziah assembled Judah and appointed them according to their fathers' households under commanders of thousands and commanders of hundreds throughout Judah and Benjamin; and he took a census of those from twenty years old and upward and found them to be 300,000 choice men, able to go to war and handle spear and shield. He hired also 100,000 valiant warriors out of Israel for one hundred talents of silver. But a man of God came to him saying, 'O king, do not let the army of Israel go

with you, for the LORD is not with Israel nor with any of the sons of Ephraim. But if you do go, do it, be strong for the battle; yet God will bring you down before the enemy, for God has power to help and to bring down.' Amaziah said to the man of God, 'But what shall we do for the hundred talents which I have given to the troops of Israel?' And the man of God answered, 'The LORD has much more to give you than this.'" (2 Chronicles 25:1-10).

Forgetting the lessons of history, King Amaziah tried to act in a political and military alliance with the northern army of Israel in order to overthrow their (Edomite) enemy. He bought their support. They were to become an army of mercenaries – people who go to war for money. But again, God pointed out that Judah was to stand alone, because Israel had turned away spiritually from God. Putting a stop to this alliance, which Amaziah had attempted in error, resulted in Amaziah losing a lot of money (100 talents of silver) as well as suffering their retaliation. What's the shared truth that this historical episode can teach disciples today? It is surely that wrong actions can prove expensive. We waste money, time and energy when we expend them in ventures which don't have the Lord's approval. But even if we lose money or lose face by abandoning them, our loss will be more than worth it if we allow ourselves to be guided back into ways more pleasing to the Lord.

God's thoughts are not our thoughts nor are our ways his ways (see Isaiah 55:8,9). His are much more beneficial for us than our own schemes. He wants to give us much more than we could ever achieve for ourselves. No one ever loses what they give up for Jesus' sake. Jim Elliott, the missionary who gave his life in reaching out to the Auca Indians, put it like this: 'He is no fool who gives away what he cannot keep in order to gain what he cannot lose.' These are true words, but few of us can say them with the same conviction he did. But, we find in them an echo of our Lord's own words: *"For whoever wishes to save his life will lose it; but whoever loses his life for My sake will find it. For what will it profit a man if he gains the whole world and forfeits his soul? Or what will a man give in exchange for his soul?"* (Matthew 16:25-26).

A person, in some sense, may gain the world – or at least gain its approval. The world, as we say, may lie at his feet as he or she reaches celebrity status and fabulous wealth. Some, a very few, even achieve world adulation – but is even that worth very much? The message once addressed to King Amaziah comes back to mind again: 'The Lord has much more to give you than this.' Freddie Mercury was someone who achieved world adulation late last century as the lead singer of the symphonic rock group, Queen, but he also was the one to ask the question: 'Does anyone know what we're living for?'

By contrast, the Bible gives us the worthy example of Moses. Raised in Pharaoh's palace, he was skilled in all the learning of those times. The world lay at his feet, but Moses came to realize that the God who is in heaven had designs for his life which amounted to much more than all of that:

> *"By faith Moses, when he had grown up, refused to be called the son of Pharaoh's daughter, choosing rather to endure ill-treatment with the people of God than to enjoy the passing pleasures of sin, considering the reproach of Christ greater riches than the treasures of Egypt; for he was looking to the reward"* (Hebrews 11:24-26).

He knew God had much more to give him than all the wealth Egypt could provide. The message *"the Lord has much more to give you than this"* can surely apply at any time in our Christian experience. God has given us every blessing in Christ, that's true, but how much are we really experiencing? We can never afford to be satisfied with our current level of discipleship.

I once heard of a man who won a free return ticket for an Atlantic crossing on a luxury liner. He was poor, and decided to take dried biscuits and cheese in a plastic bag to live off for the crossing. He was content to eat his meagre fare while the others dined in the fancy on-board restaurants, because he was just so glad to be on the trip of a lifetime. When he was nearly home on the return journey, he thought he'd check if he could afford to try just one meal in the high-class restaurant. He cautiously asked the waiter the price. The waiter was astonished: had he not read his ticket? All the meals were included in his free ticket!

Sometimes we Christians can end up living like that – gritting our teeth and enduring for the sake of the hope of heaven to come. We don't count the blessings that are already ours as those who are chosen, spiritually adopted, redeemed, forgiven and made heirs of glory (Ephesians 1). The blessings seem far away, and the promises don't feel all that real in the here and now. If it's like that, it's not God's fault. The Lord Jesus came that we might have life in all its fullness – not only an afterlife that's guaranteed, but also in this life finding unending personal encouragement and companionship; together with strength to cope with the trials of life; all the while knowing a sense of purpose and direction; with the supernatural ability to find joy in the strangest of places. In John chapter 15, the Lord invites us to choose a lifestyle of remaining in close contact with him day by day. A lifestyle like that is built on daily Bible reading and prayer. The result of it is a life infused with the joy of Jesus.

Often, we don't access all our spiritual blessings to live in conscious enjoyment of them, perhaps because we get weighed down with the common difficulties of life. But God has freely provided these things for us, that we might with his help overcome our present challenges. The encouragement from the life of Amaziah is to access the God of the much more. There's much more to Christianity than salvation from the penalty of our sins. In our life of service there's always much more of God's unlimited resources for us to appreciate – as well as the thrill and privilege of what we can be for God in his kingdom and house on earth. Perhaps it's time we read our 'ticket' again? All the details are in God's Word, the Bible.

Whenever we're tempted to wonder if denying ourselves worldly pleasures is worth it or even necessary, we should also count the cost of not doing so. What we're talking about is not so much divesting ourselves of benefits in the here and now, but investing in treasure that's eternal, stored up in heaven for us.

10

Uzziah: Who Holds Me Accountable?

God only ever has flawed people in his service. After his death, an investigation found credible evidence of a long pattern of abusive behaviour by one of the most recognizable figures in American Christianity for decades. The report found that the apologist pressured massage therapists at a spa he co-owned to perform sexual acts. It also uncovered a collection of explicit photos in his possession. When it comes to figuring out how and why, all the signs point to a lack of accountability. In due course, his board of directors apologized for their responsibility in never holding him accountable. He'd grown to be above whatever rules and the safeguards they had.

The Apostle Paul wrote to Titus: *"For the overseer must be above reproach as God's steward"* (Titus 1:7). Elders hold other elders accountable, while those in the church may bring credible accusations (1 Timothy 5:19). Spiritual leaders are called to live in accountability, with systems and people placed in their lives to safeguard against the abuse of spiritual power and positions of trust. It possibly went with the territory of being an Old Testament king that there would be little chance of being held accountable, but we do read of some who had faithful advisors and who were wise enough to take their counsel. For a while, king Uzziah was one of them …

"And all the people of Judah took Uzziah, who was sixteen years old, and made him king in the place of his father Amaziah … He continued to seek God in the days of Zechariah, who had understanding through the vision of God; and as long as he sought the LORD, God prospered him. Now he went out and warred against the Philistines … God helped him against the Philistines … The Ammonites also gave tribute to Uzziah, and his fame extended to the border of Egypt, for he became very strong. Moreover, Uzziah built towers in Jerusalem at the Corner Gate and at the Valley Gate and at the corner buttress and fortified them. He built towers in the wilderness and hewed many cisterns, for he had much livestock, both in the lowland and in the plain.

He also had plowmen and vinedressers in the hill country and the fertile fields, for he loved the soil. Moreover, Uzziah had an army ready for battle, which entered combat by divisions according to the number of their muster … who could wage war with great power, to help the king against the enemy. Moreover, Uzziah prepared for all the army shields, spears, helmets, body armor, bows and sling stones. In Jerusalem he made engines of war invented by skillful men to be on the towers and on the corners for the purpose of shooting arrows and great stones. Hence his fame spread afar, for he was marvelously helped until he was strong" (2 Chronicles 26:1,5-11,14-15).

So what we've read told us that Uzziah overthrew the Philistines, Arabians and others. He reduced Ammon to tribute. He improved agriculture; he reorganised the army; and introduced engines of war for throwing stones. He was an expert agriculturalist and a military genius. Basically, he succeeded at whatever he tried. In all we've read about King Uzziah there's one verse that's pivotal. It's the verse that says Uzziah was marvelously helped until he was strong.

Paul tells us that when we're weak, we're strong. He said in 2 Corinthians 12:10, *"I am well content with weaknesses, with insults, with distresses, with persecutions, with difficulties, for Christ's sake; for when I am weak, then I am strong."* But King Uzziah proves that the opposite is also true: when we're strong, we're weak. Paul added elsewhere: *"... let him who thinks he stands take heed that he does not fall. No temptation has overtaken you but such as is common to man; and God is faithful, who will not allow you to be tempted beyond what you are able, but with the temptation will provide the way of escape also, so that you will be able to endure it"* (1 Corinthians 10:12-13). Seemingly, Uzziah didn't take the way of escape, and so we read that:

> *"[Uzziah's] fame spread afar, for he was marvelously helped until he was strong. But when he became strong, his heart was so proud that he acted corruptly, and he was unfaithful to the LORD his God, for he entered the temple of the LORD to burn incense on the altar of incense. Then Azariah the priest entered after him and with him eighty priests of the LORD, valiant men. They opposed Uzziah the king and said to him, "It is not for you, Uzziah, to burn incense to the LORD, but for the priests, the sons of Aaron who are consecrated to burn incense. Get out of the sanctuary, for you have been unfaithful and will have no honor from the LORD God." But Uzziah, with a censer in his hand for burning incense, was enraged; and while he was enraged with the priests, the leprosy broke out on his forehead before the priests in the house of the LORD, beside the altar of incense.*

Azariah the chief priest and all the priests looked at him, and behold, he was leprous on his forehead; and they hurried him out of there, and he himself also hastened to get out because the LORD had smitten him. King Uzziah was a leper to the day of his death; and he lived in a separate house, being a leper, for he was cut off from the house of the LORD. And Jotham his son was over the king's house judging the people of the land" (2 Chronicles 26:15-21).

We all need 'valiant men' like those priests – faithful friends who'll hold us accountable for our actions; not those who indulge someone out of respect for their office or status and flatter them along with the crowd. When someone is acting in a way that's clearly contrary to the teaching of the Word of God, they really do need to be challenged in a way that's biblical – regardless of any position of authority they occupy.

Uzziah's mistake is a lesson for us all, especially if we think we're spiritually strong. We can never lose our eternal salvation, but what a disaster to be cut off from the privileges of God's house on earth in terms of our service here – as Uzziah was. The king was a leper until the day he died. Perhaps that seems a harsh punishment. Was it such a terrible thing for the king to want to offer incense to God upon the temple altar of incense? We remember that Moses was denied entry into the promised land for striking the rock instead of speaking to it (Numbers 20). Nadab and his brother were consumed by fire because they offered incense using unauthorized fire that likely hadn't come from the copper altar (Leviticus 10). Uzzah was struck down for handling the ark of the covenant when apparently trying to stabilize it (2 Samuel 6). What all these things teach us is this: when God gives detailed commands, it's important for us that we pay attention to the details.

From King Uzziah also we would do well to learn the significance of disobedience in seemingly small things. God may not act today in summary judgement as in the days of the Old Testament, but his actions then show us his unchanging attitude today if we should in a similar way be dismissive of what we might be tempted to regard as minor issues in the apostles' teaching found for us in the New Testament writings. How tragic if we should choose to ignore as irrelevant any Bible teaching for today, with the result that, like Uzziah, we deny ourselves the experience of service connected with God's earthly house!

If accountability is one major issue that this story of King Uzziah teaches us, then another is that we shouldn't seek after the gift or role of someone else. Remember, Uzziah, the king, tried to act as if he were also the priest. That was not his role. I'm reminded of the incident at the end of John's Gospel when: *"Peter turned around and saw the disciple whom Jesus loved following them ... upon seeing him, said to Jesus, 'Lord, and what about this man?'"* (John 21:20-21). Why did Peter do that? It was none of his business. But occasionally, we too may be tempted to make comparisons.

Paul says: *"... we do not presume to rank or compare ourselves with some of those who commend themselves; but when they measure themselves by themselves and compare themselves with themselves, they have no understanding"* (2 Corinthians 10:12). Then Paul adds elsewhere (to the Galatians): *"But each one must examine his own work, and then he will have reason for boasting, but to himself alone, and not to another. For each one will bear his own load"* (Galatians 6:4-5). God has works prepared for each of us to do for him (Ephesians 2:10). We should be content with discovering and delivering on those – even letting others hold us accountable!

About Hayes Press

Hayes Press (www.hayespress.org) is a registered charity in the United Kingdom, whose primary mission is to disseminate the Word of God, mainly through literature. It is one of the largest distributors of gospel tracts and leaflets in the United Kingdom, with over 100 titles and many thousands dispatched annually. In addition to paperbacks and eBooks, Hayes Press also publishes Plus Eagles' Wings, a fun and educational Bible magazine for children, and Golden Bells, a popular daily Bible reading calendar.

Notes

JOTHAM: HOW TO LIVE AN UNBLEMISHED LIFE?

1   "Dear Lord and Father of Mankind" by John Greenleaf Whittier (1807-1892)

2   "Be Still, My Soul" by Katherine von Schlegel

DAVID: HOW TO RESOLVE MARITAL CONFLICT?

3   See "The 5 Love Languages" by Dr. Gary Chapman

AHAZ: WHAT IF THINGS LOOK BETTER ELSEWHERE?

4   Letters to the Church, David C. Cook

JOSIAH: WHAT IS TRUE REVIVAL?

5   https://prosperitymedia.com.au/how-many-emails-are-sent-per-day-in-2023/).

About the Author

Born and educated in Scotland, Brian worked as a government scientist until God called him into full-time Christian ministry on behalf of the Churches of God (www.churchesofgod.info). His voice has been heard on Search For Truth radio broadcasts for over 40 years (visit www.searchfortruth.podbean.com) during which time he has been an itinerant Bible teacher throughout the UK. His evangelical and missionary work outside the UK is primarily in Belgium, The Philippines and South East Central Africa. He is married to Rosemary, with a son and daughter.

Also by Brian Johnston

Brian has published over 100 books as part of the Search for Truth ministry.

Going the Distance - How to Avoid a Spiritual Knock-out
The picture of a boxer that Paul uses in 1 Corinthians 9:26-27 is especially apt, as experience teaches us that we don't need to go very far in the Christian life before we start taking 'blows' or 'hits.' In another place, Paul talks about being "struck down."Sadly, for many today the 'knock-out' rate is high. This book brings together some notable 'sucker punches' that often get thrown at Christians - discouragement, guilt, failure, anxiety, distraction, lust, anger, pride, doubts, greed, divisions and disappointments. It aims to help us to draw on the resource of the Bible's guidance to enable us to keep our guard up.

A Test of Commitment

An interesting mix of Bible stories and modern anecodotes provides a stimulating challenge to the reader: A Glass of Wine (Jeremiah), Scribbling and Salivating at the Doors of the Gate (David), A Vineyard in Jezreel (Naboth), A Love That's Real, The Proceeds of a Property Deal (Ananias and Sapphira), The Snare of the Devil, Ten Silver Coins and a Suit (The Young Levite), Two Mules' Load of Earth (Naaman), Bread and Water in the Prophet's House (Jeroboam), A Different Kind of Fire (Nadab and Abihu), A Second Ephod (Gideon), A Piece of Brass (Hezekiah), Seven Locks of Hair (Samson), The Bleating of Sheep (Saul), Love for the World (Demas)

Only in Paul's letters to Timothy do we find the expression 'Man [or Woman] of God' in the New Testament – such a person would be characterized by godliness; but what is it and how do we become godly? Brian answers these vital questions across 11 engaging chapters. Also included are a series of Supplementary Study Questions on 1 & 2 Timothy under the heading "Dealing with the Local Church."